SHEEP WON'T SLEEP

by Judy Cox

illustrated by

Nina Cuneo

Holiday House ● New York

Clarissa could not sleep. She tried everything: warm milk, reading, humming a lullaby—even her knitting. "Counting sheep usually works," she thought.

So she closed her eyes and pictured gentle, woolly, white sheep sailing over a stile with the perfect grace of ballet dancers.

One by one, Clarissa counted them: "One
. . . two . . . three . . . four . . . five . . . six . . .
seven . . . eight . . . nine . . . ten."

A loud *baa* made her open her eyes, and to her surprise, she saw ten sheep in her room.

"It's not working," she said, watching the sheep, which had begun to get into her things. One ewe balanced on the bookcase with the lampshade on its head.

"You're not trying hard enough," advised the sheep.
"Try pairs of alpacas."

Clarissa knew that pairs meant twos, so she started to count by twos. Long-necked, long-legged alpacas leaped over the stile. Unlike the plain, white sheep, their wool was as colorful as Clarissa's basket of yarn: orange and lime green, magenta and yellow. Two by two, she counted:

"Two, four, six, eight, ten, twelve, fourteen, sixteen, eighteen, twenty!"

The alpacas joined the sheep in Clarissa's room, but Clarissa was still no closer to dreamland.

"Try llamas," said one of the alpacas, tossing a ball. "Count them by fives. That should do the trick."

So Clarissa pictured llamas, each group in a herd of five llamas. She counted llamas patterned like silly socks in polka dots, stripes, and zigzags as they scrambled over the stile and landed at the foot of her bed: "Five, ten, fifteen, twenty!"

Now her bedroom was full of woolly animals. What a racket!

"More!" said the llama. "Try yaks! Ten at a time! Just do it!"

So Clarissa shut her eyes again. Herds of yaks.
Ten in each herd. The yaks struggled over the stile,
bumping into one another. Clarissa counted by tens:

"Ten, twenty, thirty, forty, fifty!" Fifty yaks in woolly coats of many colors: argyles, diamond patterns, cables, and Fair Isles, like a wardrobe of winter sweaters.

Clarissa sneezed. Her bedroom overflowed with animals shedding wool everywhere. They *baaed*, and bleated, and snorted. They pawed and pranced—playing with her toys, reading her books, and trying on the clothes in her closet.

The walls seemed to creak and bend. The noise was terrific. And the smell! Phew!

How many animals? Clarissa added them up:

10 sheep (counted by ones)
+ 20 alpacas (counted by twos)
+ 20 llamas (counted by fives)
+ 50 yaks (counted by tens)
= 100 animals

She couldn't keep one hundred animals in her room.

19

"Maybe if I count backward, I can subtract them away," she thought. She plucked a strand of wool caught on the bedpost and began to wind it up as she counted back down from one hundred:

"Ninety-nine, ninety-eight, ninety-seven . . ."

The ball of wool in her hands grew bigger, and to her surprise, three sheep unraveled until they had completely disappeared.

She counted faster, winding the ball as she did so. One by one, she unwound each sheep. When the ball was as big as a baseball, the sheep were gone.

100-10=90

So she started on the alpacas.

90-20=70

Now the ball was as big as a basketball,
so she wound up the llamas as well.

70-20=50

Now only the yaks were left. They protested a bit
when she started winding, but soon they were gone too.

50-50=0

Now Clarissa had a gigantic ball of colorful yarn.
She got out her knitting needles.

She finished just as the morning sun peeked through the curtains. But Clarissa didn't notice. She'd been knitting all night, and now she slumbered peacefully beneath her new polka-dot, striped, zigzaggy, rainbow-patterned afghan.

For Darla and Duncan —J.C.

For my mom, who has loved my drawings from the very beginning —N.C.

Text copyright © 2017 by Judy Cox
Illustrations copyright © 2017 by Nina Cuneo
All Rights Reserved
HOLIDAY HOUSE is registered in the U.S. Patent and Trademark Office.
Printed and bound in March 2017 at Tien Wah Press, Johor Bahru, Johor, Malaysia.
The artwork was created with pen and digital ink.
www.holidayhouse.com
First Edition
1 3 5 7 9 10 8 6 4 2
Library of Congress Cataloging in Publication Data
Names: Cox, Judy, 1954– author. | Cuneo, Nina, illustrator.
Title: Sheep won't sleep : counting by 2s, 5s, and 10s / by Judy Cox ;
illustrated by Nina Cuneo.
Other titles: Sheep will not sleep
Description: First edition. | New York : Holiday House, 2017. | Summary: A girl who cannot
sleep decides to count sheep and other woolly animals by ones, twos, fives, and tens.
Identifiers: LCCN 2016051678 | ISBN 9780823437016 (hardcover)
Subjects: | CYAC: Bedtime—Fiction. | Counting—Fiction. | Wool—Fiction.| Animals—Fiction.
Classification: LCC PZ7.C83835 Sh 2017 | DDC [E]—dc23 LC record available at https://lccn.loc.gov/2016051678